Silence: The epic

Poems by

Pamela Martin

Silence: The epic
Copyright 2008 by Pamela Gowan

All rights reserved under International and Pan-American copyright conventions. No part of this book may be reproduced, stored in a retrieval system or transmitted in any form, electronic, mechanical, or by any other means, without written permission of the author.

International Standard Book Number: 978-0-615-26411-0

Cover design by Kathleen Hardy.

Table of Contents

Introduction

Part I

1.	11
2.	11
3.	11
4.	12
5.	12
6.	12
7. 11/4/08 "The Winner"	13
8.	14
9.	14
10.	14
11.	15
12.	16
13.	16
14.	16
15.	17
16.	18
17.	18
18.	18

Part II

1.	21
2.	21
3.	21
4.	22
5.	22
6.	22
7.	23
8.	24
9.	24
10.	24
11.	25
12.	26
13.	26
14.	26
15.	27
16.	28
17.	28
18.	28

Part III

1. 31
2. 31
3. 31
4. 32
5. 32
6. 32
7. 33
8. 34
9. 34
10. 34
11. 35
12. 36
13. 36
14. 36
15. 37
16. 38
17. 38
18. 38

To Lisa Muldrow

INTRODUCTION

What is the Sound of One Hand Clapping?

Even the absence of sound is sound,
which makes any onomatopoetic exploration
of silence more paradoxical than ever.
That is what this book proposes to do:
Capture the essence of sound.
Sound is like a New York minute:
It is as frenetic or placid as you make it.
As you turn each page,
listen to your life.
Turn off the television and the radio and listen.
Or,
if you wish,
leave them on. It really doesn't matter.
Just listen. What do you hear?
The distant conversation of family and friends,
the noise from the street
or the air conditioner or furnace chugging away?
And be attuned to your own thoughts racing inside your head.
I have provided blank lines
For you to jot down the "sounds of silence"
to help you remember your poems
and to realize that each time you read them
they are forever new and fresh unlike others before or hence.
Contained in these few pages
is the epic drama or story of your life as you find it
at any given moment in time.
It is the true poetry of life.

Part I

1._____

2._____

3._____

4. _____

_____
_____
_____
_____
_____
_____
_____
_____

5. _____

_____
_____
_____
_____
_____
_____
_____
_____

6. _____

_____
_____
_____
_____
_____
_____
_____
_____

7. 11/4/08 "The Winner"

I hear the murmur of the trees
And the buzzing of the bees.
I hear the cheering of the crowd.
He speaks the words that make me proud.
I hear my own exhalation
Followed by my inhalation.
Today's a day of jubilation
When we shout out exaltation!

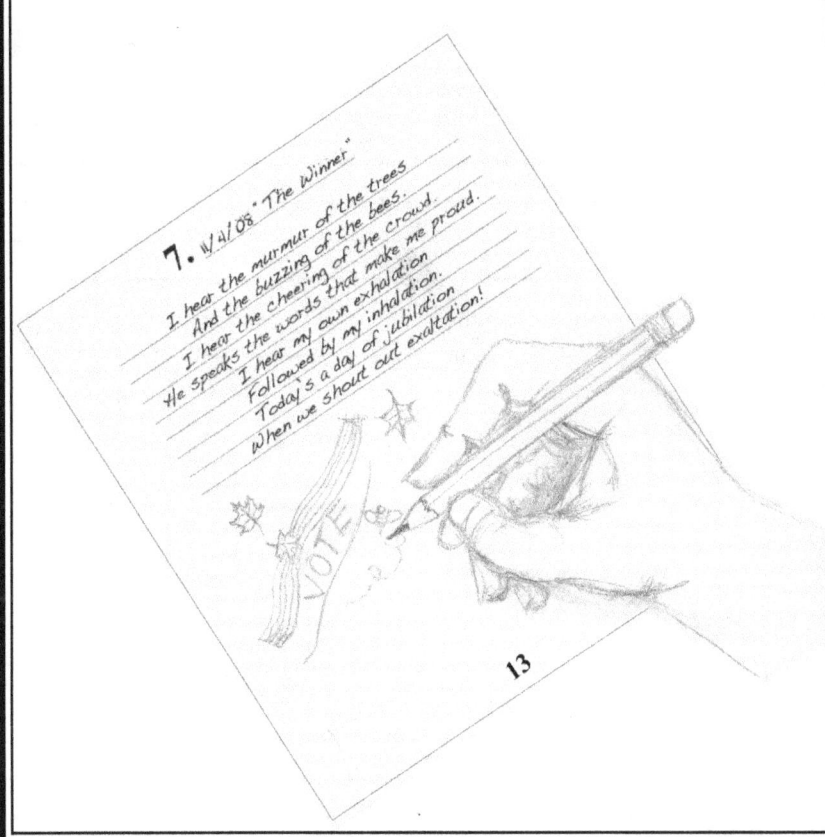

8. _____

_____
_____
_____
_____
_____
_____

9. _____

_____
_____
_____
_____
_____
_____

10. _____

_____
_____
_____
_____
_____
_____

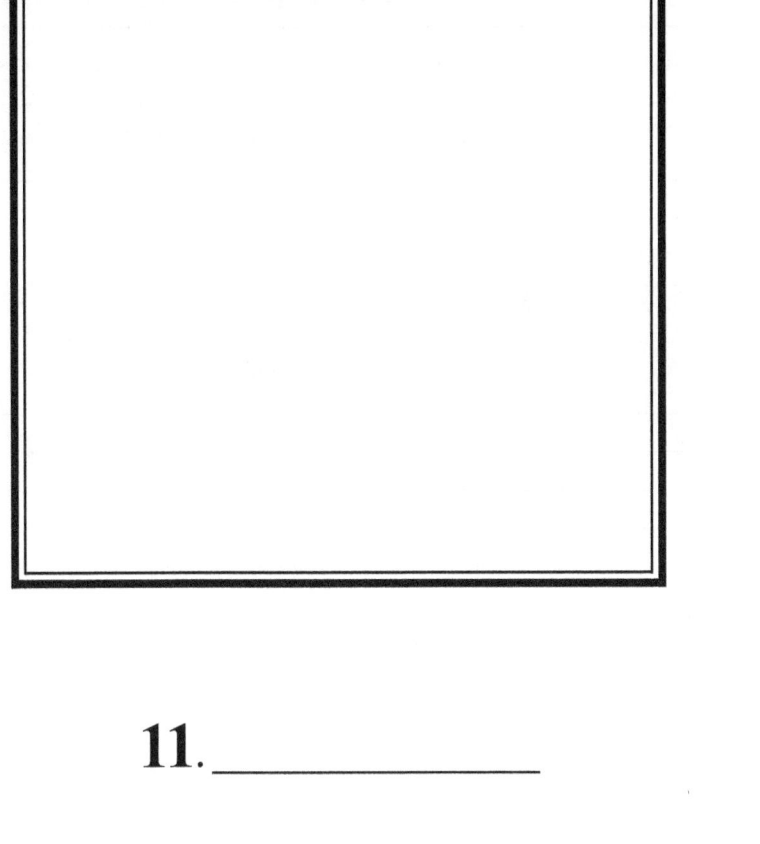

11. _____

12. _____

_____
_____
_____
_____
_____
_____
_____

13. _____

_____
_____
_____
_____
_____
_____
_____

14. _____

_____
_____
_____
_____
_____
_____
_____

15. _____

_____
_____
_____
_____
_____
_____
_____

16. _____

_____
_____
_____
_____
_____
_____
_____

17. _____

_____
_____
_____
_____
_____
_____
_____

18. _____

_____
_____
_____
_____
_____
_____
_____

Part II

1. _____

_____
_____
_____
_____
_____
_____
_____

2. _____

_____
_____
_____
_____
_____
_____
_____

3. _____

_____
_____
_____
_____
_____
_____
_____

4. _____

_____
_____
_____
_____
_____
_____
_____

5. _____

_____
_____
_____
_____
_____
_____
_____

6. _____

_____
_____
_____
_____
_____
_____
_____

7. _____

8. _____

_____
_____
_____
_____
_____
_____
_____

9. _____

_____
_____
_____
_____
_____
_____
_____

10. _____

_____
_____
_____
_____
_____
_____
_____

11. _____

_____
_____
_____
_____
_____
_____
_____
_____

12. _____

_____
_____
_____
_____
_____
_____

13. _____

_____
_____
_____
_____
_____
_____

14. _____

_____
_____
_____
_____
_____
_____

15. _____

_____
_____
_____
_____
_____
_____
_____
_____

16. _____

_____
_____
_____
_____
_____
_____
_____

17. _____

_____
_____
_____
_____
_____
_____
_____

18. _____

_____
_____
_____
_____
_____
_____
_____

Part III

1._____

_____
_____
_____
_____
_____
_____
_____

2._____

_____
_____
_____
_____
_____
_____
_____

3._____

_____
_____
_____
_____
_____
_____
_____

4. _____

_____
_____
_____
_____
_____
_____
_____
_____

5. _____

_____
_____
_____
_____
_____
_____
_____
_____
_____

6. _____

_____
_____
_____
_____
_____
_____
_____
_____
_____
_____

7. _____

_____
_____
_____
_____
_____
_____
_____
_____

8. _____

_____
_____
_____
_____
_____
_____
_____

9. _____

_____
_____
_____
_____
_____
_____
_____

10. _____

_____
_____
_____
_____
_____
_____
_____

11. _____

12. _____

_____
_____
_____
_____
_____
_____
_____

13. _____

_____
_____
_____
_____
_____
_____
_____

14. _____

_____
_____
_____
_____
_____
_____
_____

15. _____

_____
_____
_____
_____
_____
_____
_____

16. _____

_____
_____
_____
_____
_____
_____
_____

17. _____

_____
_____
_____
_____
_____
_____
_____

18*. _____

_____
_____
_____
_____
_____
_____
_____

*It goes without saying.

Notes

Notes

Notes

Notes

Notes

Notes

Notes

Notes

www.ingramcontent.com/pod-product-compliance
Lightning Source LLC
Chambersburg PA
CBHW031218090426
42736CB00009B/967